Getting Ready for Space

By Carmen Bredeson

Consultants
Minna Gretchen Palaquibay
Rose Center for Earth and Space
American Museum of Natural History
New York, New York

Nanci Vargus, Ed.D.
Primary Multiage Teacher
Decatur Township Schools
Indianapolis, Indiana

Dr. Jeanne Clidas
National Literacy Consultant

Children's Press®
A Division of Scholastic Inc.
New York   Toronto   London   Auckland   Sydney
Mexico City   New Delhi   Hong Kong
Danbury, Connecticut

Designer: Herman Adler Design
Photo Researcher: Caroline Anderson
The photo on the cover shows astronaut Story Musgrave making a final space suit check.

Library of Congress Cataloging-in-Publication Data

Bredeson, Carmen.
  Getting ready for space / by Carmen Bredeson.
     p. cm. — (Rookie read-about science)
Includes index.
Summary: A simple overview of the training that astronauts go through for missions on the space shuttle.
  ISBN 0-516-22498-0 (lib. bdg.)   0-516-26953-4 (pbk.)
  1. Astronauts—Training of—Juvenile literature. [1. Astronauts. 2. Space shuttles.] I. Title. II. Series.
  TL850 .B74 2003
  629.45'07—dc21
                                    2002011196

Astronauts (AS-truh-nauts)
go to school just like you.
They learn how to live and
work in space.

Everything floats in space.
New astronauts take an
airplane ride to see how
this feels.

The plane flies up, up, up,
and then dives. When it
dives, the people inside
float.

5

The plane goes up
and down many times.
This makes some people
sick.

That is why the
plane is nicknamed the
"Vomit Comet."

Astronauts also work in mock-ups. Mock-ups are machines that look like the real space shuttle.

In mock-ups, astronauts practice what they will do in space.

The crew learns how to strap themselves into their seats. They practice using packets of food and the oven. They try out the shuttle bathroom, too.

12

Many of the mock-ups
have computers. The
crew goes over their plans
again and again. They are
getting ready for their trip
to space.

Each space shuttle has a robot arm. The astronauts learn to use this long arm. They move it up and down, back and forth.

15

The robot arm lifts
big things in space. The
astronauts can even ride on
the arm when they work.

Astronauts wear space
suits when they take
space walks. They practice
putting on the big suits.
It is quite a job.

19

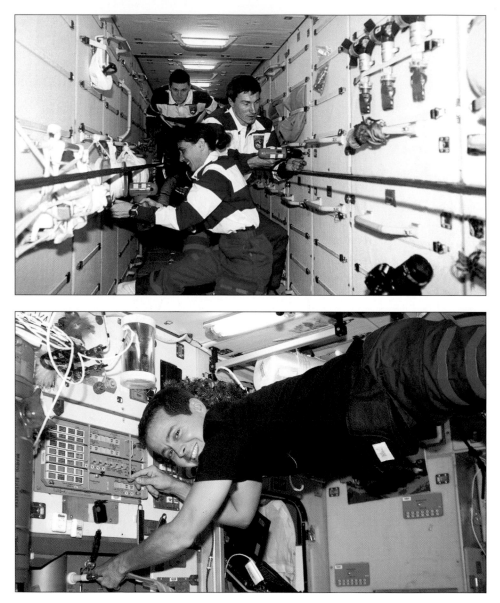

There is a lot of work to do on a space flight. It is hard to use tools when you are floating.

When you turn a screwdriver, you might turn instead of the tool.

Floating in space feels a
lot like being underwater.
Astronauts get used to
this feeling by working
in a swimming pool.

23

24

The men and women put on space suits. They are lowered into the water. They put things together and take them apart.

The big day is here!
The astronauts are on
the real space shuttle.

Five, Four, Three, Two,
One, Liftoff!

The crew finally gets to see what space is really like.

Would you like to float high above Earth?

Words You Know

astronaut

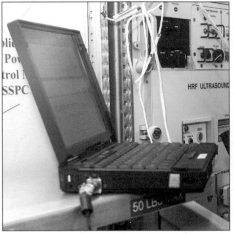
computer

mock-up

robot arm

space shuttle

space suit

Index

About the Author

Carmen Bredeson has written dozens of nonfiction books for children. She lives in Texas and enjoys traveling and doing research for her books.

Photo Credits

Photographs © 2003: Corbis Images: cover, 8, 15 bottom, 25, 30 bottom, 31 bottom right (Roger Ressmeyer), 5 (Jim Sugar); NASA: 3, 7, 11, 12, 15 top, 16, 19, 20 bottom, 20 top, 23, 24, 27, 28, 30 top left, 30 top right, 31 top, 31 bottom left.